Keeping Safe

Ryan Wheatcroft   Katie Woolley

Published in paperback in Great Britain in 2019 by Wayland

Copyright © Hodder and Stoughton, 2018

Editor: Victoria Brooker
Designer: Anthony Hannant, Little Red Ant

ISBN: 978 1 5263 0560 2

10 9 8 7 6 5 4 3 2 1

Wayland, an imprint of
Hachette Children's Group
Part of Hodder and Stoughton
Carmelite House
50 Victoria Embankment
London EC4Y 0DZ

An Hachette UK Company
www.hachette.co.uk
www.hachettechildrens.co.uk

Printed and bound in China

Contents

Wonderful World

The world is an exciting place — there are woods to run in, cities to explore, new people to meet and games to play.

Not everything in your world is safe, and sometimes accidents can happen.

Learning how to keep safe at home, outdoors, on roads and online will help you to explore your world safely.

At Home

Accidents can happen around the house. If you're not careful, sharp tools such as knives and scissors can cut you. When using these items, keep the sharp edge away from your body.

In the kitchen, ovens and hobs get very hot. They can burn your skin. Make sure an adult is nearby when you are cooking. Always wear oven gloves if you need to touch hot pans or dishes.

Out and About

Riding your bike or scooter is great fun. Wearing a helmet is important because it will protect your head if you fall. It should fit snugly and the chin straps should be tight so the helmet can't slip off.

When you are out and about, be careful near roads. Bright clothes with reflectors will help other people on the road to see you.

On the Road

Cars, motorbikes and buses go very fast, which can make crossing a road difficult. Look for a safe place to cross, such as a zebra crossing. Don't try to cross between two parked cars as it's hard to see around them.

Before you step into the road, stop, look and listen!
Wait until there is a gap in the traffic and start
walking. Keep looking left and right. Do not run
as you cross the road.

Stop ...

look ...

listen.

Near Water

Swimming, splashing and paddling are all good fun, but water can also be dangerous. It may be fast moving or be deeper than it looks. Knowing how to stay safe around water is very important.

Never go near water without an adult.
Wear clothes to keep you safe, such as
armbands when you are learning to swim,
or a life jacket when you are in a boat.

Whatever the Weather!

Help your body to stay safe all year round!
On hot days, the sun can quickly burn your skin.
Wearing sun cream will help to protect it.
Wear a hat so your head doesn't burn and
to keep you cool.

When the weather is cold, wrap up in lots of layers to keep warm. If it's snowing, wear shoes with a good grip to keep you steady.

What's In Your Mouth?

Be careful about what you put in your mouth. Never put small toys or cleaning items in your mouth. Don't pick berries without checking with an adult first.

Medicines can make you feel better when you are sick, but they can be dangerous. Too much medicine, or the wrong sort of medicine, can make you unwell. Don't help yourself to medicines without checking with an adult.

Safety Online

The internet is a useful tool. It can help you with school projects, you can read about your favourite pop star or email your best friend. When you are online, you need to stay safe. Here are some top safety tips!

Never share your password — not even with friends.

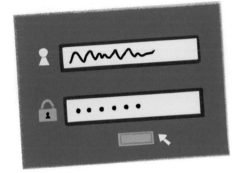

Don't talk to strangers online or accept friend requests from strangers.

Think carefully about what you post on social network sites.

Never share personal information, such as your name, school and age or where you live.

Ask an adult to check your privacy settings.

Always log out of a website on any device when you have finished using it.

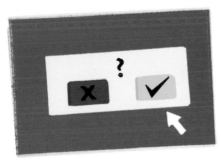

If in doubt, or you don't feel safe, tell an adult you trust!

Stranger Danger

Strangers are people you don't know. Most strangers aren't dangerous but some might be. If a stranger tries to talk to you, walk away and tell an adult.

If you get lost or separated from family and friends, find an adult you trust to help you. This could be another parent with children or a police officer. Tell them your name, your parents' names and phone number and where you live.

My Body, My Rules!

Your body belongs to you. It's up to **YOU** if you want to be hugged, hold hands with a friend or play tickling games with your brothers and sisters.

People should never see or touch a part of your body that can be covered by a swimsuit. If you feel unsure, it's okay to say 'No!' and find an adult that you trust.

Friends or Foes?

It is not just your body that can get hurt. People can hurt your feelings, too. Friends are always kind to each other. Bullies are people who are unkind and can hurt your feelings.

Bullying may happen at home, at school and even online. Bullying is wrong. If you are being bullied, talk to an adult.

Emergency, Emergency!

Parents, carers and teachers all help you to learn about keeping safe. There are other people who can keep you safe, too. Doctors and nurses make you feel better when you are sick, police officers stop criminals and firefighters put out fires.

Accidents do happen and sometimes you need to take action quickly in an emergency! If someone is badly hurt or in danger, and you need help straight away, call 999.

Top Safety Tips!

Always wear a helmet when riding your bike. It should cover your forehead and the straps should be fastened tightly under your chin.

Talking about safety is an important way of being prepared and keeping yourself and others safe.

Listen to adults you trust and always follow instructions.

To keep you safe from strangers, walk to school with a friend. When you play outside, choose safe spots that are well lit and with lots of people about.

If you are lost or need help, ask an adult you trust such as a police officer or another parent.

When travelling in a car, always wear your seat belt and sit on a booster seat.

Teachers' and Parents' Notes

This book is designed for children to begin to learn about the importance of being healthy, and the ways in which we can keep safe when we are at home and out and about. Read the book with children either individually or in groups. Don't forget to talk about the pictures as you go.

The world is a busy and exciting place for children. There are lots of activities to do, places to explore and people to meet. Learning how to stay safe at all times is very important. Here are some discussion topics to encourage further thinking about keeping safe:

 What can you do if you don't feel safe?

 Can you think of any people who help you keep safe?

 Do you and your family have rules that help you stay safe online? What are they?

 What is the difference between a friend and a bully?

Activities you can do:

 Draw the tip of an iceberg above the ocean's waves and the rest of the iceberg under the surface. Draw a computer screen on the tip of the iceberg. Explain that a computer screen is like the tip of an iceberg — you can't see what's going on below. Write on the iceberg, under the sea, all the things children can think of that are not seen on an internet chat forum, for example what someone looks like, where they live etc.

 Create a collage from pictures in magazines, newspapers and from the internet that tells someone else all about staying safe.

Further reading

Dot.Common Sense by Ben Hubbard *(Watts, 2018)*
Keeping Safe (Healthy and Happy) by Robyn Hardyman *(Wayland, 2016)*
Staying Safe Online (Kids Get Coding) by Heather Lyons and Elizabeth Tweedale *(Wayland, 2016)*

Glossary

accident an event that doesn't happen on purpose. An accident can result in damage or an injury.

armbands bands worn around the arm to help someone swim

emergency a dangerous situation

life jacket an inflatable jacket that keeps a person afloat in the water

medicine a drug or treatment that makes someone feel better

online to be connected to a computer and using the internet

password a secret word or phrase that must be used to gain entry to a specific place, account or webpage

reflectors a piece of metal or glass that reflects light so a bike or a person can be seen in the dark when light shines on it

zebra crossing part of the road painted with white stripes, where vehicles must stop when someone wishes to cross the road

Index